Real-World Math

Grades 5–6

Strengthen the Math Skills Needed in Everyday Life

by Susan Carroll

Carson-Dellosa Publishing Company, Inc.

Greensboro, North Carolina

Credits

Editor
Susan Morris

Layout Design
Jon Nawrocik

Artists
Van Harris
Jon Nawrocik

Cover Design
Annette Hollister-Papp

Cover and Inside Photos
Photo www.comstock.com
© 1993 Digital Wisdom, Inc.
© 2001 Brand X Pictures All rights reserved.
© 1999 EyeWire, Inc. All rights reserved.
© Photodisc
© Corbis Images
© 2004 Dynamic Graphics, Inc.

Printed in the USA • All rights reserved.

ISBN 1-59441-054-2

Table of Contents

About This Book...

Math is everywhere!

Real-World Math was written to connect mathematics to real-world problems that students encounter in their daily lives. The activities in this book are designed to help students become independent problem solvers as they use patterns, elapsed time, calendars, measurement, money, and other mathematical concepts to solve problems.

The book contains 14 activities that focus on real-world problems. While using the picture at the beginning of each activity as a reference, students can demonstrate problem-solving skills by answering the questions on the following pages. Copies of each picture should be provided for the students. Each picture is followed by two activity pages with short-answer and multiple-choice questions. The first activity page is geared toward lower-level thinking skills while the second activity page progresses through higher-level thinking. The two different formats allows you to differentiate how to use the activity for the varying learning levels of students.

A teacher notes and extensions section follows each activity. Each section includes a description of the picture that students will use to complete the worksheets. Review this description with students prior to having them complete the worksheets. The teacher notes contain teaching strategies and ideas for instruction. For example, Caring for Roses (page 16) has suggestions for teaching ratios to students learning the skill for the first time. Foreign Exchange (page 20) gives strategies to convert one country's currency to another. The teacher notes are designed to use as needed. In addition, theme-based extension activities are included. These activities are intended to give other options for expanding students' knowledge on the subject or providing cross-curricular connections. For example, Fragrant Fund-Raisers (page 36) suggests that students research different fund-raising opportunities for their school. Students must choose a fund-raising product that meets consumers' needs while making the most money for their school. Using these ideas allows you to extend students' knowledge, as well as vary the activities according to students' needs.

As students use the activities in this book, they will begin to make more mathematical connections to the world in which they live. They will see that math truly is everywhere.

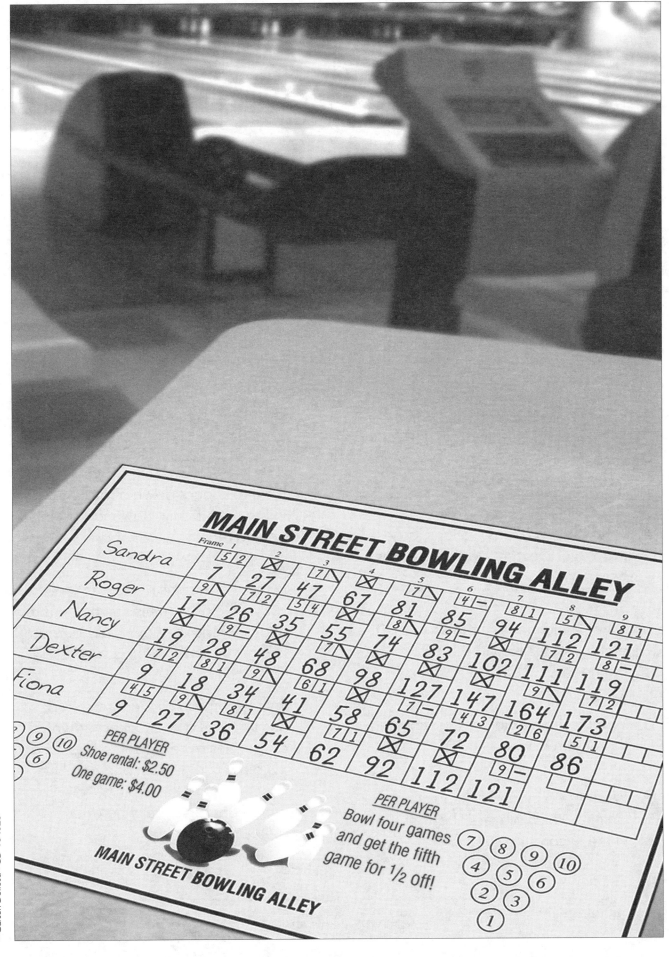

Right Up Your Alley

Use the bowling scorecard and price list to answer the questions.

1. A spare is indicated with a /. A strike is indicated with an X. What is the difference between the total number of strikes and spares?

2. In the fifth frame, which 2 players have scores that total 155?

3. Roger was ahead of Sandra in the first frame but lost the lead in the second frame. In which frame did he regain his lead? By how many points?

4. In which frame was Nancy's largest lead over Dexter? How large was her lead?

5. What is the mean of the scores in the eighth frame? (Round the answer to the nearest 10th.)

6. What is the median of the scores in the eighth frame?

7. What is the mode of the second frame? Which players had that score in the second frame?

8. If Nancy bowls 1 strike in the 10th frame, what percentage of her frames contain strikes?
   a. 40%   c. 60%
   b. 50%   d. 70%

9. What fraction of the frames Fiona has bowled are strikes or spares?
   a. $\frac{1}{2}$ c. $\frac{1}{4}$
   b. $\frac{1}{3}$ d. $\frac{1}{5}$

10. If Fiona knocks down a total of 8 pins in the ninth frame, how many points behind Nancy will she be?

11. In the 10th frame, if Dexter knocks down 7 pins with his first ball and his final score is 95, how many pins did he knock down with his second ball?

12. In the tenth frame, Sandra rolled her first ball and knocked down all of the pins except for the 9, 6, and 10 pins. With her second ball, she knocked over the 9 pin. What would Sandra's score be after the 10th frame?

CD-104025 • Real-World Math

Name _____

Right Up Your Alley

Use the bowling scorecard and price list to answer the questions.

1. In the second frame, Dexter knocked down these pins with his first ball: 1, 2, 3, 4, 5, 6, 8, and 9. The pins left standing are called a split. What fraction of the remaining pins did he knock down with his second ball?
   - a. $\frac{1}{2}$
   - b. $\frac{1}{3}$
   - c. $\frac{1}{4}$
   - d. $\frac{1}{5}$

2. In bowling, a turn in which no pins are knocked down is represented by a —. Of all turns shown on the scorecard, what is the percentage of turns in which no pins were hit? Remember that a strike counts as 1 turn.
   - a. 20%
   - b. 10%
   - c. 8%
   - d. 5%

3. If each bowler listed on the scorecard pays for shoe rental and 2 games, what does each player pay?

4. If each bowler on the scorecard pays for shoe rental and 2 games, what is the total cost for all 5 bowlers?

5. If 5 players brought their own shoes and bowled 3 games, how much money would they pay altogether?

6. If all 5 players rented shoes and bowled 5 games, how much money would they spend altogether?

7. If all 5 players brought their own shoes and bowled 5 games, how much money did they save by bringing their own shoes?

8. Sandra brought her own bowling shoes, and Nancy rented shoes. They each bowled 6 games. How much more money did Nancy spend than Sandra?

9. If all 5 players bowled 6 games and wore their own shoes, how much money would they spend altogether?

10. Roger bowled 4 games and wore his own shoes. Fiona bowled 3 games but rented shoes. Which player spent more money?

11. The bowling alley is having a special. The first player pays full price, second player pays $\frac{3}{4}$ of the price, third player pays $\frac{1}{2}$ of the price, fourth player pays $\frac{1}{4}$ of the price, and fifth player plays free. How much does it cost for all 5 players to play 1 game?

Right Up Your Alley

The Picture:

The picture is a scorecard used in bowling. There are five players playing the game. The game is not complete. It is Fiona's turn in the ninth frame. The scorecard shows standard bowling pin placement and features game and shoe rental prices, as well as a special discount for bowling five games.

Teacher Notes:

Teach students the basics of reading a bowling scorecard:

- For each game, a person has 10 turns. Each turn is scored in a *frame*.
- In each frame, a person has two chances to knock down all 10 bowling pins.
- The numbers recorded on the scorecard represent the number of pins knocked down in each frame. These numbers are added across the page to determine the final score. For example, Dexter knocked down nine pins in his first frame. In the next frame, he knocked down nine pins, which resulted in a total score of 18 for Dexter's second frame (9 + 9 = 18).
- When a player knocks down some pins in the first roll of a frame and knocks down the remaining pins in the second roll, it is called a *spare*. A spare is indicated with a / on the scorecard.
- When a player knocks down all 10 pins in the first roll of a frame, it is called a *strike*. A strike is indicated with an X on the scorecard.
- A turn in which no pins are knocked down is represented by a – on the scorecard.

When explaining *mean*, *median*, and *mode* to students, help them remember the difference by teaching them the definitions listed in the Teacher Notes section of Buy the Book (page 40).

Extension Activities:

1. To teach students the specifics of scoring and playing a bowling game, have the class read *Bowling for Beginners: Simple Steps to Strikes and Spares* by Don Nace (Sterling, 2002).
2. After students have completed activity #1, call a local bowling alley and ask for game and shoe rental prices. Have students calculate how much it will cost them to visit the bowling alley, rent shoes, and play one game each. Then, take them on a field trip to the bowling alley. Assign groups of five students and allow them to play each other. Encourage students to use what they learned to score the games. (Before completing this activity, ask families' permission and inquire about students' abilities to lift heavy objects.)
3. Have students read two fiction books about the subject of bowling, such as *The Million Dollar Strike* by Dan Gutman (Hyperion, 2004) and *The Case of the Haunting of Lowell Lanes* by Angela Elwell Hunt (Here's Life Pub., 1992). Then, have the class compare the books using a Venn diagram.
4. Teach students bowling vocabulary. For example, the *pit* is the space at the end of the lane where balls and pins are collected. The *gutter* is the area on each side of the lane that guides the ball into the pit when it leaves the lane. The *return* is the track on which pins roll from the pit to the ball rack. The *ball rack* is the place where balls are stored before they are rolled and after they return from the pit. When a bowler is unable to knock down all 10 pins in a single frame, it is called an *open frame*. When the 7 and 10 pins are the only pins left standing, it is called a *split*. When a bowler receives two strikes in a row, it is called a *double*. Three strikes in a row is called a *turkey*.

← ✈ Gates 26-50   🧳 A B Baggage | 🧳 C D Baggage   6-25 Gates ✈ ↗

SA Arrivals SA

Flight	City	Time	Status	Gate		Flight	City	Time	Status	Gate
147	Atlanta	3:15 p	Delayed	B 42		140	Miami	3:15 p	At Gate	B 17
1063	Boston	7:30 p	On Time	C 12		303	Newark	3:45 p	On Time	C 24
170	Charlotte	3:12 p	At Gate	B 18		2876	New Orleans	4:00 p	On Time	C 11
300	Chicago	3:10 p	Delayed	D 15		16	New York	3:05 p	Delayed	A 19
1855	Dallas/Ft. Worth	3:07 p	Delayed	D 24		36	Orlando	3:53 p	On Time	C 30
924	Denver	5:15 p	On Time	C 29		902	Philadelphia	4:30 p	On Time	B 15
501	Honolulu	6:25 p	On Time	B 18		45	Phoenix	6:00 p	On Time	A 21
1059	Houston	4:35 p	On Time	A 25		10	San Francisco	3:10 p	At Gate	D 35
86	Las Vegas	3:15 p	At Gate	D 6		246	Seattle	2:55 p	Delayed	D 18
473	Los Angeles	3:00 p	Delayed	A 37		827	Washington, D.C.	3:20 p	Delayed	A 7

To reduce congestion in the airport, please meet your party at baggage claim.

TOSHIMI

SA Departures SA

Flight	City	Time	Status	Gate		Flight	City	Time	Status	Gate
152	Atlanta	3:45 p	Delayed	B 37		145	Miami	3:45 p	At Gate	B 12
1068	Boston	4:20 p	On Time	C 7		308	Newark	4:15 p	On Time	C 19
175	Charlotte	3:50 p	At Gate	B 13		2881	New Orleans	4:30 p	On Time	C 06
305	Chicago	3:40 p	Delayed	D 10		21	New York	3:35 p	Delayed	A 14
1860	Dallas/Ft. Worth	3:37 p	Delayed	D 19		41	Orlando	4:23 p	On Time	C 25
929	Denver	5:45 p	On Time	C 24		907	Philadelphia	5:00 p	On Time	B 10
506	Honolulu	6:55 p	On Time	B 8		50	Phoenix	3:40 p	Boarding	A 16
1064	Houston	5:05 p	On Time	A 20		15	San Francisco	3:40 p	At Gate	D 30
91	Las Vegas	3:45 p	Boarding	D 1		251	Seattle	3:25 p	Delayed	D 13
478	Los Angeles	3:30 p	Delayed	A 32		832	Washington, D.C.	3:50 p	Delayed	A 2

All passengers should report to their gates at least 15 minutes before boarding.
Boarding will begin 15 minutes before flights are scheduled to depart.

TOSHIMI

When Is My Flight?

Use the airline flight schedule to answer the questions.

1. Parker's mother is arriving from Denver. Parker is flying to Denver on the next flight. How much time is there between her arrival and his departure?

2. Sarah is in a hurry because her flight is leaving soon. She can't remember what time it departs. A gate agent is helping her search the board. What time does boarding begin for flight 91?

3. Dante is on flight 924. He needs to catch flight 506. If he plans to arrive at the gate for his flight 15 minutes before departure time, how much time does he have to eat dinner?

4. Megan is traveling to Charlotte. What time does she need to report to the gate?
   a. 3:20 P.M.   c. 3:35 P.M.
   b. 3:30 P.M.   d. 3:50 P.M.

5. Carmen works at the passenger check-in desk. Her shift starts at 3:25 P.M. If she works until the last plane on the schedule departs, what time will her shift end?

6. Pascal's flight to Atlanta was delayed 1 hour and 20 minutes. What time will his flight leave for Atlanta?

7. Airport management wants to keep track of how many flights are on time. What fraction of afternoon flights are scheduled to arrive on time?
   a. $\frac{9}{10}$ c. $\frac{1}{2}$
   b. $\frac{9}{20}$ d. $\frac{10}{20}$

8. Due to bad weather, some flights had delayed arrival times. What percentage of flights were delayed?

9. George is in charge of concourse B. His job is to keep track of how many flights are arriving and departing. What fraction of the flights are leaving from concourse B?
   a. $\frac{1}{2}$ c. $\frac{1}{4}$
   b. $\frac{1}{3}$ d. $\frac{1}{5}$

10. Captain Rogerson flew in from Orlando. His next flight is to Denver. How long is his layover?

11. Ricky is in charge of gate B18. How much time does he have between flights to complete his paperwork?

When Is My Flight?

Use the airline flight schedule to answer the questions.

1. Mr. Suarez is the airport manager. He is in charge of overseeing the entire airport. If there are 50 gates in each lettered concourse, how many total gates does he manage?

2. Mr. Suarez makes sure the airport is running smoothly by keeping track of how many flights have landed. What fraction of flights have already arrived at the gates?

3. Jackie is on the delayed flight from Los Angeles. What is the latest her flight can be before her connecting flight to Charlotte begins boarding?

4. It is now 4:13 P.M. Jamison's flight should have started boarding 5 minutes ago. Which flight is he on?

5. Steven's flight to Dallas was delayed $1\frac{1}{2}$ hours. The flight is 1 hour and 45 minutes long. What time will he arrive in Dallas?

6. Logan is waiting to board flight 305. If the plane is delayed for 1 hour and 45 minutes, what time will Logan's flight depart?

7. Mr. Suarez must file a report about how many people missed connecting flights because their arriving flights were late. At the end of the afternoon, 259 people had missed connecting flights. What is the average number of passengers per delayed flight that missed connecting flights?

8. Mr. Suarez also keeps track of day-to-day changes. On an average day, 25% of arriving flights are delayed. According to all flights listed, by what percent is today's percentage higher or lower than average?

9. Bill and Phil process all passengers checking in for flights that are scheduled to depart between 3:00 P.M.–4:00 P.M. If an average of 100 passengers fly on each plane, approximately how many passengers did Bill and Phil check in?

10. The last flight from Phoenix arrived at 2:45 P.M. How much time is between the flights arriving from Phoenix?
    a. 2 hrs. 15 min.   c. 3 hrs. 15 min.
    b. 3 hrs.   d. 3 hrs. 30 min.

When Is My Flight?

The Picture:

The picture is two airline flight schedules; one is for arrivals, and one is for departures. It contains 20 cities that are listed in alphabetical order. Information included on the schedules is flight numbers, cities' names, times of arrival or departure, status, and gate numbers. There is additional information on the schedules that tells when to arrive at the gates and when flight boarding will begin. The status of the flights gives additional information:

Arrivals: The city listed is the flight's city of origin.
- On time—the plane is in flight and is scheduled to land on time.
- Delayed—the plane is delayed from its previous destination.
- At gate—the plane has arrived and is currently at the gate.

Departures: The city listed is the flight's destination city.
- On time—the plane is scheduled to leave on time.
- Delayed—the plane will not be leaving the airport at its scheduled time.
- At gate—the plane is at the gate but has not started boarding passengers.
- Boarding—the flight is boarding passengers and is within 15 minutes of the flight's departure time.

Teacher Notes:

When teaching elapsed time to upper elementary students, have them convert hours and minutes to a whole number by multiplying the number of hours by 60, then adding additional minutes. Then, have them subtract the whole numbers. Finally, have them divide the answer by 60 to find the amount of hours elapsed. Explain that the remainder will be the number of additional minutes.

Extension Activities:

1. Have students choose vacation destinations to visit from the cities listed on the schedule. Have them plan itineraries that include departure times for them to leave for their destinations and arrival times for them to return home. They can include hotels and activities, as well as the duration of their vacations.
2. Have students visit Web sites for commercial airline flights. Provide an itinerary for a virtual trip that includes a schedule for hotel check-in times or an appointment they must attend. Have them try to find the flight schedule that best meets their travel needs.
3. Have a discussion with students about different time zones around the world. Explain that crossing time zones may affect arrival times and departure times for connecting flights. For example, discuss how a person could travel for two hours and land in a city where it is only one hour later than when he departed his original city.
4. Have students look at the flight schedules to see if they notice a pattern between arrival gates and departure gates assigned to the same city. Additionally, see if they notice a pattern between arrival and departure flight numbers.

Caring for Your Roses

The following instructions are ideal for caring for roses, but roses will do fine with less work. Just remember, the more you give your roses, the more they will give you!

CHOOSING A SITE:

- **Good Drainage**—Roses love water but will die of root rot in soggy soil. Dig a 2' x 2' (61cm x 61cm) hole and fill with water. If it drains within an hour, fill again. If no water remains after an hour, you have a well-drained site. If not, the easiest solution is to use raised beds.
- **Good Air Circulation**—Make sure your plants are spaced apart for air to circulate through and around them. If using a trellis, make sure it is wide enough for multiple climbing stalks. This helps dry the plants quickly to prevent black spots, mildew, etc.
- **Good Soil**—Soil needs to be prepared so that the plants can take in nutrients. The ideal mix is ¼ each of clay, manure, compost, and sand. Till or dig 8"–10" (20 cm–25 cm) deep. Add the four different types of soil and dig another shovel head length to mix. Till again and rake smooth. (A mixture of ½ bagged soil conditioner and ½ dirt from the ground can also be used.)

YOU ARE NOW READY TO:

- **Plant**—Roses can be planted any time of year as long as the ground is not frozen. Check the approximate mature size of the bushes you will plant and space accordingly. Dig a hole twice the size of the pot. Add ⅓ cup 0–46–0 triple super phosphate, ⅓ cup dolomite, and 2 cups alfalfa pellets. Split the plastic container and carefully remove the rose bush with the soil and root ball intact. Place in the hole with the soil of the root ball even with the top of the hole. Fill with remaining soil mixture, firming down soil with your hand to eliminate air pockets. DO NOT firm down the soil with your feet, or the soil will be too compacted.
- **Water**—Slowly give the bush 5 gallons (19 liters) of water. Repeat every 5–7 days unless there has been at least 1" (2.54 cm) of rainfall. From November through March, water at least once a month.
- **Mulch**—Apply a 4"–6" (10 cm–15.25 cm) layer of fine pine bark mulch within 2" (5 cm) of the bush base. This will hold moisture, reduce weeds, and keep the ground around the rose bush at a more constant temperature. You may also use compost, manure, or grass clippings.
- **Feed**—Apply liquid fertilizer every two to three weeks—1 gallon (3.8 liters) for small bushes, 3 gallons (11.5 liters) for larger ones. Use ½ strength the first year. Do not fertilize after September 15 to allow plants to go into a dormant state.
- **Prune**—Avoid cutting the long stems the first year to allow leaves to grow. Remove spent blooms as soon as possible to prevent hips from forming. Stop pruning in October to help bring about winter dormancy. Prune to keep desired size.

Caring for Roses

Use the directions to grow roses to answer the questions.

1. Do you have a well-drained site to plant roses if water remains after 130 minutes?

2. If $\frac{1}{4}$ of your ideal mix of soil is sand, what fraction is manure and clay?
   a. $\frac{1}{4}$ c. $\frac{1}{3}$
   b. $\frac{1}{2}$ d. $\frac{2}{3}$

3. Kathy bought 5 roses in 10-inch diameter pots and 5 roses in 8-inch diameter pots. If she has planted three 10-inch pots and two 8-inch pots, how many holes are left to dig, and how wide are the holes?

4. Martel planted 5 large and 5 small rose bushes on March 1. If he fertilizes them on the 1st and 16th of the recommended months during the year, how many gallons of liquid fertilizer will he use through September 15?

5. Louisa used liquid fertilizer on each of her 36 large rose bushes. How many total liters of liquid fertilizer did she use if her plants were 3 years old?
   a. 108 gallons   c. 108 liters
   b. 414 gallons   d. 414 liters

6. Kelly planted 20 small rose bushes. How many gallons of liquid fertilizer did she use in the first 2 months if she fertilized the plants every 2 weeks?

7. David and Jessica are planting 17 rose bushes. How much triple super phosphate, dolomite, and alfalfa pellets do they need?

8. Parker spaced his plants 50 cm apart for good air circulation. How many inches apart did Parker plant his roses? (Round to the nearest whole number.)
   a. 10 inches   c. 20 inches
   b. 15 inches   d. 25 inches

9. Bill is taking care of Robin's prize-winning rose bush. There is a drought, and it hasn't rained in weeks. He waters the plant for the entire month of June, and the drought continues through the end of the month. If he waters the rose bush every 5 days, how many gallons of water does he use?

10. Thomas is pruning the roses in July. How many more months will he prune the roses before he should stop to allow winter dormancy?

Name _____

Caring for Roses

Use the directions to grow roses to answer the questions.

1. If you apply $\frac{1}{2}$ foot of pine bark mulch at the base of the rose bush, how many centimeters is that?

2. When Sarah planted her small rose bush, she used 50% of the recommended strength of liquid fertilizer. How many liters did she use?

3. There are 8 cups of alfalfa pellets in a box. What percentage of the box of pellets would you use if you plant 3 rose bushes?
   a. 25%   c. 50%
   b. 40%   d. 75%

4. Bart made a mixture of 1:1:6 of triple super phosphate, dolomite, and alfalfa pellets. How many rose bushes does he plan to plant?

5. Carlos is trying to determine how large a hole to dig for his new rose bush. If the radius of the potted rose is 10 cm, what is the diameter of the hole you should dig?
   a. 10 cm   c. 30 cm
   b. 20 cm   d. 40 cm

6. Cara added the liquid fertilizer to the water in her watering can. If she is fertilizing her small rose bush for the first time, how many cups of fertilizer should she add to the watering can?

7. How many times a month should the plants be watered if there has not been at least 1 inch of rainfall?

8. Martha is planting a rose bush. What ratio of bagged soil conditioner to dirt from the ground should she use?

9. Roses will continue to need water during winter. What percentage of the year should you water your plants at least once a month?
   a. 5%   c. 21%
   b. 42%   d. 84%

10. Johan is digging the holes for the roses he bought for his mother. He bought 5 rose bushes in 8-inch pots. What was the diameter of the hole he dug to plant each rose bush?

Caring for Roses

The Picture:

The picture is directions for growing roses.

Teacher Notes:

A *ratio* is a comparison by division of two quantities with the same units. A ratio can be written as a fraction, decimal, or percent. It can also be written with a colon between the two numbers being compared. For example, when making the ideal soil mixture, the directions tell you to combine ¹/₄ cup of four different ingredients. This can also be written as 0.25 cup of each ingredient, 25% of the mixture, or 1:1:1:1.

To find the diameter of the hole in comparison to the radius of the pot the rose comes in, have students double the radius to get the diameter of the pot, then double the pot's diameter to make the correct diameter of the hole.

Have students use given conversions of measurement for other conversions. For example, students are given the information that 1 inch is equal to 2.54 cm. They can use this information for other standard length conversions by multiplying the number of given inches by 2.54.

Extension Activities:

1. Have students use graph paper to design a raised bed or garden for roses. Students should include appropriate spacing between each rose bush for root growth and air circulation.
2. Plant flowers in clay pots for a school fund-raiser. Have students create the ideal soil mixture for the plants using clay, manure, sand, and compost.
3. When creating the ideal soil mixture, let students change the ratios of ingredients and plant similar plants in the different mixtures. Have them record if there is any difference in the growth of the plants. Have students graph the growth of each plant every two days by measuring the tallest point of the plant.
4. Visit a local home improvement store, farmers' market, or nursery where roses are sold. Have students write down the varieties sold. Then, let them make a Venn diagram of the varieties the different stores had in common.
5. Plant several varieties of roses on the school's campus. Have students track the number of blooms each plant produces. After the first year, compare the data with blooms counted the previous year.
6. Use different store-bought liquid fertilizers on rose bushes of the same variety. Have students note the growth, then determine which brand promotes the most growth and the most blooms.

Today's Exchange Rates

Country	Currency	Amount of Currency Equal to One U.S. Dollar
Argentina	Peso	2.89
Australia	Dollar	1.29
Austria	Euro	0.77
Brazil	Real	2.53
Canada	Dollar	1.24
China	Yuan Renminbi	8.28
Denmark	Kroner	5.74
Egypt	Pound	5.80
France	Euro	0.77
Germany	Euro	0.77
Greece	Euro	0.77
Hong Kong	Dollar	7.80
India	Rupee	43.79
Iraq	Dinar	1,458.60
Italy	Euro	0.77
Japan	Yen	105.87
Kenya	Shilling	105.84
Mexico	Peso	11.11
New Zealand	Dollar	1.39
Poland	Zloty	3.27
Russia	Ruble	27.75
Spain	Euro	0.77
Sweden	Krona	7.06
Switzerland	Franc	1.19
Thailand	Baht	39.59
United Kingdom	Pound	0.53
Vietnam	Dong	15,840.00
Zambia	Kwacha	4,612.50

Foreign Exchange

Use the currency conversion chart to answer the questions.

1. Eric is flying to Brazil. He exchanges U.S.$20.00. How many reals is this?

2. Dinah bought her dinner at a diner with 14,586 dinars. In what country was Dinah having dinner, and how much was her dinner in Canadian dollars?

3. Ramone bought a soda and a cookie. His total was 31,680 dong. How much is that in U.S. dollars?

4. In Mexico City, Mexico, you would like to purchase a Mexican frazada (blanket) for 90 pesos. You have U.S.$8.00 to spend. Do you have enough to buy the blanket?

5. Hong has 20 yuan renminbi. Franz has 25 euros. Who has more money in Canadian dollars?

6. Pamela traveled from Italy to Spain with 65 euros. She went to the bank to exchange her currency. How much of what type of currency did she leave the bank with?

7. Is 1 United Kingdom pound worth more or less than 1 U.S. dollar?

8. In Paris, France, a souvenir of the Eiffel Tower is 7.70 euros. How many U.S. dollars are needed to buy the souvenir?

9. In Moscow, Russia, Nadia paid 800 rubles for a warm hat. Will C$30.00 be enough to buy the hat?

10. In Tokyo, Japan, there are many bargains at the 100 Yen Store. Max bought a postcard, candy, and a belt for 300 yen. How many U.S. dollars did he spend?

11. Christos paid U.S.$17.98 to take a country mountain tour in New Zealand. What was the local price of the tour?
    a. NZ$17.99   c. NZ$35.98
    b. NZ$12.94   d. NZ$24.99

12. Would you make more money getting paid 118.77 baht per hour or C$3.25 per hour?

Foreign Exchange

Use the currency conversion chart to answer the questions.

1. Including the United States, what percentage of the countries on the chart use dollars as their currencies? (Round to the nearest whole number.)
    a. 5%   c. 50%
    b. 17%   d. 72%

2. Yesterday, the value of the euro was equal to 0.81. Did the euro gain or lose value overnight?

3. The United Kingdom has not agreed to replace its currency with the euro. Does their pound have a lesser or greater value than the euro?

4. Melanie wanted to visit the great Egyptian pharaoh exhibit at a museum in Canada. A ticket to the museum is C$15.00. How much would the ticket price have been if the exhibit had been held in the pharaoh's home country?

5. Paco traveled from Australia to New Zealand. If he had A$300.00, how much did he have in New Zealand dollars after he converted his money?

6. Maya had U.S.$171.00 before she left for her trip to Zambia. She spent 15% of her money on meals in the airport. How much money did she have after exchanging her money to the local currency?
    a. 25.65 kwacha
    b. 145.35 kwacha
    c. 670,426.87 kwacha
    d. 788,737.50 kwacha

7. Hector wanted to travel to a place where the currency exchange was not too different. Which 2 foreign currencies are closest to having the same value in U.S. dollars?

8. Cassidy bought a doll from a Russian dealer on the Internet. The dealer converted the price to C$25.00. What was the original cost in rubles?

9. Which currency is worth about $\frac{3}{4}$ of the U.S. dollar?

10. Freddie noticed there were two countries that used the peso for their currency. Which country's peso has a greater value in the United States?

Foreign Exchange

The Picture:

The picture is a currency conversion chart. It shows 28 countries in alphabetical order. A currency chart like this would be displayed at a bank or at an airport in a city that has international tourism.

Teacher Notes:

Explain that to exchange U.S. dollars for foreign currency, students should:

1. Look at the exchange rate for the country whose currency they are converting to.
2. Multiply the amount of foreign currency that is equal to one U.S. dollar by the number of U.S. dollars.
   For example:
   U.S.$4.00 = ? euros
   U.S.$1.00 = 0.77 euros
   4.00 x 0.77 = 3.08 euros
   U.S.$4.00 = 3.08 euros

Explain that to exchange foreign currency for U.S. dollars, students should:

1. Look at the total amount of the foreign currency they want to convert to U.S. dollars.
2. Divide that number by the amount of foreign currency that equals U.S.$1.00. The answer is the value in U.S. dollars.
   For example:
   5.40 euros = ? U.S. dollars
   0.77 euros = U.S.$1.00
   5.40 ÷ 0.77 = U.S.$7.01
   5.40 euros = U.S.$7.01

Explain that to exchange foreign currency for another foreign currency, students should:

1. Convert the foreign currency to U.S. dollars using the second method described above.
2. Convert the U.S. dollars to the other foreign currency using the first method described above.
   For example:

15 pesos = ? Canadian dollars	U.S.$1.35 = ? Canadian dollars
15 pesos = ? U.S. dollars	U.S.$1.00 = U.S.$1.24
11.11 pesos = U.S.$1.00	1.35 x 1.24 = C$1.67
15 ÷ 11.11 = U.S.$1.35	15 pesos = U.S.$1.35 = C$1.67

Extension Activities:

1. Have a multicultural fair. Help students create or bring in different goods from around the world. Let them convert each item's price from one country's currency to another.
2. Have students design an international board game that is similar to Monopoly®. Instead of U.S. destinations, have them create a game board that includes different places in the world. Houses and hotels can be replaced with monuments found in the cities. Have students write game cards that require them to convert money to move ahead.
3. Have students visit a Web site for currency conversions. Assign one currency to each student to track for a month. Have students create charts from their data to show how the values of their assigned currencies fluctuate daily.

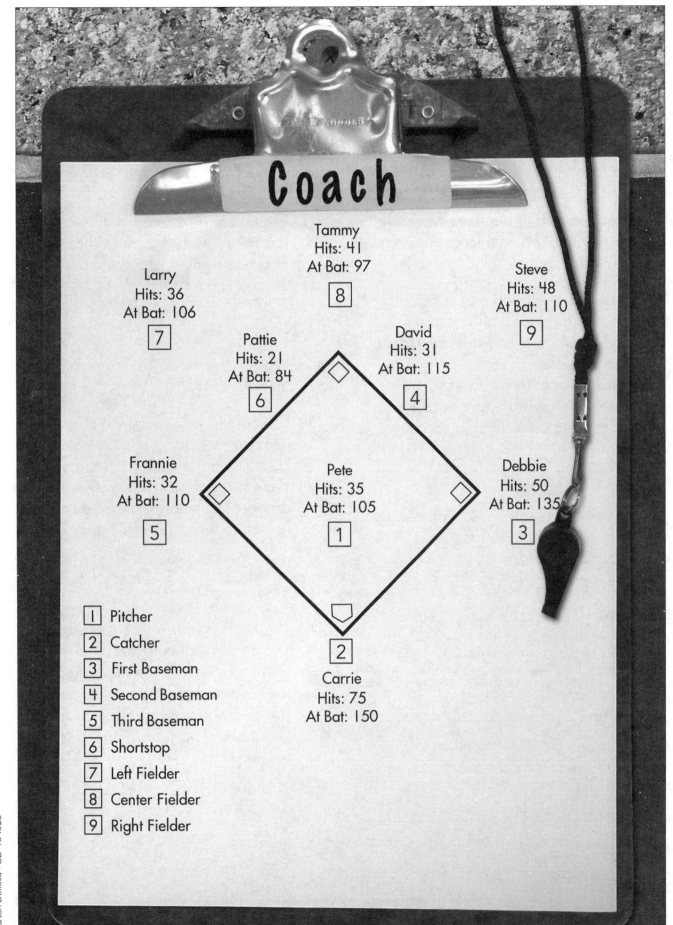

Coach

Tammy
Hits: 41
At Bat: 97
8

Larry
Hits: 36
At Bat: 106
7

Steve
Hits: 48
At Bat: 110
9

Pattie
Hits: 21
At Bat: 84
6

David
Hits: 31
At Bat: 115
4

Frannie
Hits: 32
At Bat: 110
5

Pete
Hits: 35
At Bat: 105
1

Debbie
Hits: 50
At Bat: 135
3

2

Carrie
Hits: 75
At Bat: 150

1 Pitcher
2 Catcher
3 First Baseman
4 Second Baseman
5 Third Baseman
6 Shortstop
7 Left Fielder
8 Center Fielder
9 Right Fielder

Batter Up!

Use the field position chart to answer the questions.

The coach uses the field position chart and the information on it to calculate a variety of statistics.

For questions 1-9, use the players' statistics to calculate their batting averages. Batting average is calculated by dividing a player's number of hits by the number of times at bat. Round all batting averages to the nearest thousandth and write them as decimals.

1. Pete _____

2. Carrie _____

3. Debbie _____

4. David _____

5. Frannie _____

6. Pattie _____

7. Larry _____

8. Tammy _____

9. Steve _____

10. The coach is calculating statistics for the entire team, too. What is the average number of hits for the entire team?
   a. 75   c. 48
   b. 21   d. 41

11. What is the mode for the number of times at bat?

12. The coach is deciding which players need more batting practice by calculating how many times they did not get a hit when they were batting. How many times did Frannie not get a hit when she was at bat?

13. Which of the players got a hit $\frac{1}{3}$ of the times at bat?

14. The team is entering a tournament. The coach wants to see where his team stands by comparing the team's overall batting average to the averages of the other teams. What is the batting average for the entire team?

Batter Up!

Use the field position chart to answer the questions.

The coach is choosing the starting lineup. He wants the player with the fourth highest number of hits to bat first, the player with the third highest number of hits to bat second, and so on. Write the names of the starting 4 players in the correct batting order.

1. _____

2. _____

3. _____

4. _____

5. What is the median number of hits for the entire team?

6. How many times was David at bat when he did not get a hit?

7. The coach has given the team a challenge this season to see who can get more hits, the boys or the girls. Who is winning so far?

8. Which player had more at bats without getting a hit: Tammy or Pattie?

9. The team is halfway through the season. If they set a goal to increase the number of hits they've achieved thus far by 83%, how many hits will they have by the end of the season?
   a. 83   c. 306
   b. 675   d. 452

10. Steve had 25% more hits this time last year than he does this year. How many hits did he have this time last year?

11. The average number of times a player has been at bat is 6 times per game. Using this average, about how many games has Pattie played in this season?
    a. 12   c. 6
    b. 14   d. 84

12. Which 3 players have a combined total of 113 hits?

Batter Up!

The Picture:

The picture is a baseball coach's field position chart. The chart contains players' field positions as well as the number of hits and at bats they have received so far this season.

Teacher Notes:

Explain that *batting average* is calculated by dividing a player's number of hits by the number of times at bat. Have students write batting averages as decimals that have been rounded to the nearest thousandth.

Discuss how to calculate the following:
* *Mean*, also called the average, is the sum of numbers in a set divided by the number of addends.
* *Median* is the middle number in a set of numbers. To calculate median, arrange numbers in a set in order from lowest to highest value. Then, count to the middle.
* *Mode* is the number found most frequently in a set of numbers.

Explain how to convert decimals to fractions and percents:
* Fraction to a decimal: Divide the numerator by the denominator.
* Decimal to a fraction: Remove the decimal point and write the number as the numerator. The denominator should be a multiple of 10, depending on the place the last digit of the decimal occupies. For example, if the decimal is 0.235, then the denominator is 1,000 because the last digit of the decimal occupies the thousandth place. The fraction can then be reduced to lowest terms.
* Fraction to a percent: Divide the numerator by the denominator, then move the decimal point two places to the right.
* Decimal to a percent: Move the decimal two places to the right.

Extension Activities:

1. Have students use real baseball cards to calculate players' batting averages.
2. Have students research past and present baseball players. Let them compare batting averages, salaries, number of games played per season, etc., and record the differences and similarities on a Venn diagram.
3. If your town has a local major or minor league team, try to arrange a family night or a class field trip to the ballpark.
4. Have students compare the major league ballparks. Search the Internet for Web sites that give information about when stadiums were built, seating capacities, and dimensions of the fair play areas. Help students conclude that while the dimensions of the infield may be the same, each ballpark is uniquely different.
5. Have students research baseball players who are members of the Baseball Hall of Fame. Let students compare players' batting averages, number of games attended, number of home runs, and other records.

THE BLUEBIRD

Appetizers

Mozzarella Cheese Sticks	3.95
Potato Soup	2.00
Vegetable Soup	2.00
Potato Skins	3.25
Nachos	3.75
Combination Platter	6.25

(includes any three appetizer choices)

Sandwiches

All sandwiches include your choice of side item—french fries, onion rings, cottage cheese, or applesauce. Add 99¢ to substitute a baked potato. Sandwiches come with your choice of toppings (tomato, lettuce, cheese, and onion).

Hamburger 5.95
a quarter pound of beef
Chicken 5.50
a juicy grilled breast
Chicken Deluxe 6.00
deep-fried and topped with cheese and bacon
Fish 5.75
catfish (deep-fried or broiled)

Salads

Salads include bread sticks or garlic bread.

House Salad 3.20
topped with cheese and croutons
Chicken House Salad 4.20
topped with grilled chicken
Fried Chicken Salad 4.20
topped with fried chicken
Spicy Salad 4.95
topped with spicy grilled chicken or beef

From the Grill

Items ordered from the grill include: a house salad, biscuits or rolls, and two sides. Side items are applesauce, cottage cheese, baked potato, potato soup, vegetable soup, corn, or green beans.

Filet 13.00
10-ounce steak, prepared to your liking
Baby Filet 11.00
6-ounce steak, prepared to your liking
Pork Chops 9.55
two 5-ounce chops–spicy, grilled, or plain
Chicken 8.85
two 5-ounce breasts–covered in barbecue sauce or plain
Sirloin 9.00
10-ounce steak, prepared to your liking

Pasta

Pasta is served with a house salad and your choice of bread sticks or garlic bread.

Spaghetti 6.75
with marinara or meat sauce
Lasagna 8.15
vegetable or meat
Magnificent Chicken 7.95
pasta topped with chicken and a light cheese sauce

Children's Menu

These items are for children 12 and under.

Chicken Fingers	2.95
Grilled Cheese Sandwich	1.95
Hot Dog	1.75
Hamburger	2.25
Turkey Sandwich	2.00

Desserts

All desserts are large enough to share. We recommend one dessert for every two people.

Ice Cream 3.25
vanilla, chocolate, strawberry, or chocolate chip (Add 50¢ for topping–chocolate or caramel.)
Homemade Pie 3.75
Ask your server for tonight's selection.
Cheesecake 4.00
served with cherry or strawberry topping

Name _____

Let's Do Lunch

Use the menu to answer the questions.

1. You and your parents order soup and Chicken Deluxe sandwiches. You and your mom both get baked potatoes with your meals. What is your total lunch bill without tax and tip?

2. How many different appetizer combination platters are possible?

3. How many different choices do you have for paying your bill at The Bluebird?

4. Baxter does not eat beef, pork, or chicken, but occasionally he eats seafood. What fraction of sandwiches, salads, and pasta dishes can he eat?

5. How many different side items are available on the menu?

6. A friend called and said that she was running late. She told you to order for her. You know she likes salad and meat but not spicy food. What percentage of the salads could you order for her?

7. You are buying your friend a gift certificate to The Bluebird. His favorite dish is the Magnificent Chicken, and he loves cheesecake for dessert. What value of gift certificate should you purchase? (Round to the nearest dollar.)

8. You and 2 friends went to The Bluebird for sandwiches. If your total was $18.89 before tax, what did you and your friends order?

9. How many different combinations of sandwiches and sides can you have?
   a. 5   c. 15
   b. 10   d. 20

10. Kathryn had an order of potato skins, a house salad, a sirloin, and a dish of strawberry ice cream. How much was her order?
    a. $16.05   c. $15.50
    b. $18.70   d. $16.25

11. What fraction of items that contain chicken cost less than $5.00?

Name _____

Let's Do Lunch

Use the menu to answer the questions.

1. How many possible ice cream and topping combinations are there for $3.75?
   a. 8   c. 12
   b. 10   d. 14

2. Mario had potato soup and grilled pork chops. He bought a slice of pie to take home. What was the total of his menu items?

3. Seth split a sirloin steak with his brother. They bought an additional house salad. How much did it cost each of them to eat if they split the check equally?

4. For how many different menu items might you be asked your choice of dressing for a salad?

5. Taylor does not like onions. How many different ways can he order his chicken deluxe sandwich with the remaining topping choices?
   a. 4   c. 6
   b. 5   d. 7

6. A hamburger on the children's menu is $\frac{1}{2}$ the size of a hamburger on the regular menu. How many ounces is a child's hamburger?

7. The waitress spilled some food on your lap by accident. The restaurant manager only charged you 20% of the cost of your meal. If you had cheese sticks, a fish sandwich, and cheesecake, what was your reduced total?

8. If the recommended portion of meat is 4 ounces per meal, how many recommended portions are in 1 regular filet?
   a. 1.5   c. 2.5
   b. 2   d. 3.5

9. What is the least expensive meal you can purchase if you order an appetizer, a pasta, and a dessert?

10. The Bluebird has changed its menu once every 4 years since it first opened. How many menus have they had so far?

11. You have $20.00 to spend for dinner. Choose 3 items from the menu within your budget. (Remember to include 6% sales tax and a 15% tip.)

Let's Do Lunch

The Picture:

The picture is a menu from The Bluebird restaurant. There are menu choices for several courses. The restaurant has been open for 26 years.

Teacher Notes:

When solving the problem about the possible combination of toppings for the Chicken Deluxe sandwich without onions, have students use the following permutation formula:

- Consider the possible combinations of one different topping on each sandwich:
  chicken and tomato, chicken and lettuce, chicken and cheese (3)
- Next, consider the possible combinations of two different toppings on each sandwich:
  chicken, tomato, and lettuce; chicken, tomato, and cheese; chicken, lettuce, and cheese (3)
- Then, consider the possible combinations of three different toppings on each sandwich:
  chicken, tomato, lettuce, and cheese (1)
- Finally, add the number of combinations from each group. (3+3+1= 7 possible combinations)

Some areas charge sales tax on food, while others do not. Inform students of the policy in your area and the amount of applicable sales tax.

Tipping is an important skill to teach students at a young age. Generally, there is an accepted minimum tip for full-service restaurants and a slightly lower accepted minimum tip for buffet-style restaurants. Inform students about the accepted minimums in your area.

Refer to page 24 for strategies for converting decimals, fractions, and percents.

Extension Activities:

1. Have students bring in a variety of paper menus from local restaurants. After giving them a budget, have them determine how many different combinations of meals they can order from each menu.
2. Ask local restaurants for charts that include nutritional values for their menu items. Have students create healthy meals that have fewer than 15 grams of fat or 600 calories.
3. After reviewing several local menus, have students determine how many meals are available to people with special dietary needs, such as a vegetarians, people with a lactose intolerance, or people on reduced fat diets. For restaurants that do not offer items for people with special dietary needs, have students write letters to the managers that explain possible menu items made with ingredients that are already in meals on their current menus.

C

FRIENDLY WIRELESS

Save ¼ off all calls made between 7 P.M. and 11 P.M.

555-6796
Bellview, PA

555-8296
Westchester, PA

FREE PHONE
No Monthly Charge

Long Distance $0.50 per minute

All local calls $0.30 per minute

SALE!
½ off
LONG DISTANCE
CALLS!

FREE PHONE

555-2947
Bellview, PA

LOW MONTHLY FEE ONLY $20.00 ALL LOCAL CALLS $0.10 PER MINUTE LONG DISTANCE $0.50 PER MINUTE

Cell@ebrate
Phone Company

FREE PHONE • FREE PHONE • FREE PHONE • FREE PHONE • FREE PHONE • FREE PHONE

HOLD-ON
Wireless
1-800-555-4596
1776 Independence Blvd.
Bellview, PA 29564
All local calls $0.05 per minute
One time set-up fee of $45.00 per phone
Long Distance $0.60 per minute
*Bonus! After the first 100 minutes, save 20% on all remaining minutes!

Cell Phone Rental

Cell USA 555-6759
Cell Palace 555-1936
Celli-Rentz 555-6352

Cell Service/Repair

Hailey's Wireless 555-8547
Jon's Cell Service 555-4512
Phones by Susan 555-7916
Rupert's Wireless 555-5141
Techno Wizards 555-4200
Van's Wireless 555-2574

Phone Home

Use the yellow pages ad for cell phones to answer the questions.

1. Daniel is having trouble with his cell phone service. How many companies can he call for repairs?

2. Mrs. Jarvis wanted to get an inexpensive cell phone in case of an emergency. Which phone company is best for her needs?

3. How many minutes did Justin talk to his next-door neighbor if his bill from Hold-On was $1.10 for the call?

4. Renée got her phone bill for the month. There were 97 minutes of local calls and 55 minutes of long distance. All of her calls were after 7:00 P.M. If her bill total was $43.45, which phone company did she use?
   a. Friendly   c. Cell-ebrate
   b. Hold-On   d. Hailey's Wireless

5. What is the annual fee for a Cell-ebrate phone?

6. How many phones will Hold-On set up for $315.00?

Name	Length of Call	Type of Call	Time of Call
Joan	24 minutes	long distance	3:15 P.M.
Nancy	72 minutes	local	5:30 P.M.
Susan	48 minutes	long distance	7:33 P.M.
Kathy	50 minutes	local	10:00 A.M.

Use the chart to answer questions 7–11.

7. If Nancy and Susan both use Friendly Wireless, who has the least expensive call?

8. Joan, Susan, and Nancy all use Friendly Wireless. Together, Joan and Susan talked as long as Nancy did. Which cost more: Nancy's call, or Joan and Susan's calls combined?

9. If all 4 women use Hold-On Wireless, who has the least expensive bill for her call?
   a. Joan   c. Susan
   b. Nancy   d. Kathy

10. If Susan uses Friendly Wireless, how much more would she pay for her call before 7:00 P.M.?

11. How much did Joan pay for her call if her phone company is Cell-ebrate?

Phone Home

Use the yellow pages ad for cell phones to answer the questions.

1. Cell-ebrate is only charging $\frac{1}{2}$ price for long distance calls. How much will you save per minute based on their regular charges?

2. Lucy chose Hold-On Wireless for all of her office workers. If there are 6 workers, how much is her total set-up fee?

3. You called your dad who was out of town on a business trip. You talked between 6:55 P.M. and 7:23 P.M. How much were you charged by Friendly Wireless?

4. How much more or less would you be charged for the same phone call to your dad using Hold-On Wireless?

5. What is the absolute lowest charge for 1 minute of long distance if you are charged the lowest price each company has to offer, including all discounts?

   Friendly: _____

   Cell-ebrate: _____

   Hold-On: _____

6. How many minutes of non-discounted local calls with Friendly Wireless would equal the $20.00 monthly fee of Cell-ebrate?

7. You spent 2 hours on the phone with your best friend who was on vacation 100 miles away. How many minutes will be discounted by Hold-On Wireless?

8. What would the charges be for that call to your best friend?

9. Cell-ebrate is waiving the monthly fee for 6 months for new customers. How much will a new customer save?

10. You paid $10.00 for a 20-minute, long distance call using Friendly Wireless. What time was it?
    a. 6:30 P.M.   c. 7:00 P.M.
    b. 6:45 P.M.   d. 7:15 P.M.

11. If you save 20% on your minutes with Hold-On Wireless, how much would you pay per minute for a long distance call?

Phone Home

The Picture:

The picture is a page found in the yellow pages of a telephone book. There are three advertisements for local cell phone companies that describe the per-minute rates for long distance and local calls. The ads also include additional charges for services, such as monthly and set-up fees.

Teacher Notes:

To determine the charge for a long distance or local call, students should multiply the number of minutes by the fee charged for the type of call.

To determine an annual fee, students should multiply the monthly fee by 12.

Have students calculate the price per minute using the information given in each problem. Students can determine the best price by comparing the charges from each company to find the lowest price per minute.

To find out the amount of discount for Friendly Wireless, students should determine how many call minutes occur between the hours of 7:00 P.M. and 11:00 P.M. Regular charges apply during all other hours. For example, if a person had a 10-minute phone call between 6:55 P.M. and 7:05 P.M., two separate rates would apply. Students must calculate the regular fee for the first five minutes and apply the $\frac{1}{4}$ off for the additional five minutes.

Extension Activities:

1. Gather pamphlets from local and national cell phone companies that contain their monthly and yearly rates. Have students compare the different monthly plans to find which company has the best per-minute rate for both long distance and local calls.
2. Have students use local yellow pages to find what special discounts are available for mentioning a yellow pages ad when purchasing a cell service plan or cell phone.
3. Have students compare charges for cell phone companies and home land lines. Let them determine which is more economical.
4. Have students research different cell phones. Have them try to find the best price for the phone with the most options.
5. Discuss cell phone contracts with students. Explain that companies offer larger discounts to customers who sign service agreements for longer than a year. Talk about the "fine print" and if the amount of money saved by signing a contract actually saves money in the long run.

Flowering Fund-Raisers

Fund-Raisers

Allium
Quantity: 10 bulbs
Our Price: $5.99

Begonia
Quantity: 15 tubers
Our Price: $35.99

Crocus
Quantity: 20 bulbs
Our Price: $15.99

Daffodil
Quantity: 25 bulbs
Our Price: $14.99

Dahlia
Quantity: 2 plants
Our Price: $7.99

Gladiolus
Quantity: 9 bulbs
Our Price: $7.99

Hyacinth
Quantity: 25 bulbs
Our Price: $39.99

Lily
Quantity: 15 bulbs
Our Price: $9.99

Tulip
Quantity: 40 bulbs
Our Price: $25.99

Fragrant Fund-Raiser

Use the fund-raiser catalog page to answer the questions.

1. Mrs. Brooks purchased 9 gladiolus bulbs and 10 allium bulbs. How much change did she receive if she gave you $30.00?
   a. $13.98   c. $5.99
   b. $7.99   d. $16.02

2. Which is a better bargain per bulb, 20 crocus bulbs or 9 gladiolus bulbs?

3. Would you receive a discount if you purchased 2 dahlia plants and 18 gladiolus bulbs?

4. Eli bought 1 package each of allium, dahlia, and gladiolus. About how much money did he spend?
   a. $22.00   c. $26.00
   b. $24.00   d. $28.00

5. Would it be more expensive to order 4 dahlia plants or 25 daffodil bulbs?

6. What is the fewest number of packages of lilies you need to purchase to get 100 bulbs?

7. You want to purchase the same quantity of alliums, crocuses, and tulips. How many packages of each type of flower should you order?

8. What is the total cost for 15 tubers of begonias?

9. You have $50.00 to purchase flower bulbs for your new garden. You want to buy 9 gladiolus bulbs, 20 allium bulbs, and 20 crocus bulbs. Do you have enough money to make this purchase?

10. You want to buy 1 package of flowers that you can plant in 3 equal rows. Which flowers should you buy?
    a. alliums   c. lilies
    b. crocuses   d. hyacinths

11. What is the mode of the flower prices? What is the median of the flower prices? What is the mean of the flower prices?

12. How much would it cost to purchase 1 of each package?

Fragrant Fund-Raiser

Use the fund-raiser catalog page to answer the questions.

1. What fraction of the flowers on the catalog page are available in bulbs?

2. Fabio wants to purchase exactly 30 flower bulbs. Which flower purchase would be the best deal?

3. How much would you save on your order if you purchase 25 hyacinth bulbs and 40 tulip bulbs?

4. Your personal goal is to sell at least $300.00 worth of flowers. You have sold 160 tulip bulbs. How many hyacinth bulbs would you have to sell to reach your goal?

5. Peter wants to plant a lily, a tulip, and a daffodil in each row. How many different rows can he make using the 3 flowers?
   a. 3   c. 5
   b. 4   d. 6

6. If Andrea purchases $95.00 worth of flowers, what would her total be after she received the advertised discount?

7. What percentage of the flower packages range in price from $7.99 to $15.99?

8. Your school receives 10% of every flower order during the fund-raiser. Your aunt orders 15 begonia tubers, 8 dahlia plants, 20 crocus bulbs, and 30 lily bulbs. How much will the school receive from her order?

9. Joy purchased a total of 25 bulbs. What combination of flowers could she have purchased?
   a. begonias and alliums
   b. daffodils and hyacinths
   c. lilies and alliums
   d. lilies and gladiolus

10. Bryan needs to purchase exactly 35 bulbs to plant in the Memorial Garden at school. Which would be a better bargain, 25 hyacinth bulbs and 10 allium bulbs or 20 crocus bulbs and 15 begonia tubers?

Fragrant Fund-Raiser

The Picture:

The picture is a page from a flower catalog. The flowers are sold in multi-quantity packages. There are bulbs, plants, and tubers available.

Teacher Notes:

Fund-raisers are a great way to teach students about taking purchase orders, collecting money, and persuading the consumer to purchase a product.

To calculate discounts, have students add all items to be purchased. Then, have them compare the sum to the discount list to determine the amount of discount. Let them multiply the sum by the discount percentage, then subtract the discount amount from the original sum to find the discounted price.

Have students divide the price of each package by the number of items in each package to find the price per unit.

Teach students that they can work backward, using the given factors to find the missing factors in a problem. For example, if they subtract the total dollar amount sold from the selling goal, they can determine how many more packages they need to sell to reach the goal.

Extension Activities:

1. Have students participate in a fund-raiser at school to raise money to beautify the school's campus.
2. Have students make fund-raising a class project. Students can request literature from the PTA president about fund-raising opportunities for the school. The class should choose which fund-raiser would make the most money for the school. They should compare the percentage of sales that the school will receive as well as which items will probably sell the best.
3. Set a goal for each student participating in a class fund-raiser. Use the money to purchase something for the classroom.
4. Have students order and plant bulbs for Mother's Day.
5. Keep track of daily sales from a fund-raiser on a bar graph.
6. Before a fund-raiser begins, have students predict what would be the best-seller. After a fund-raiser is over, have students test their predictions by comparing them to actual sales. Students can create a pie chart to show what percentage of their sales came from the different items sold.

WELCOME TO THE BOOK FAIR!
TOP 15 SELLERS

Book Titles	Genre	Pages	Price
1. Stevie Solves a Mystery	Mystery	110	$6.95
2. Adventures in a Small Town	Fiction	80	$5.00
3. Great Math Secrets	Nonfiction	75	$8.95
4. Roscoe and Rufus Ride Again	Fiction	33	$7.00
5. A Rhyme a Dozen	Poetry	50	$4.95
6. Taking Pictures of Your Pets	Nonfiction	92	$9.95
7. There's Something Fuzzy Under My Bed	Fiction	50	$8.95
8. Maps That Kids Will Use	Nonfiction	125	$10.95
9. Hamsters in Outer Space	Fantasy	85	$7.95
10. Why the Penguin Doesn't Fly	Legend	25	$5.95
11. Johnny Sailor: How I Became a Movie Star	Biography	98	$3.00
12. Great Recipes for Young Chefs	Cookbook	100	$9.95
13. One Mountain at a Time	Nonfiction	134	$6.95
14. Best Games to Play Inside	Entertainment	175	$11.95
15. Roger Goes on a Field Trip	Realistic Fiction	50	$5.00

Buy the Book

Use the top 15 sellers list to answer the questions.

1. Zachary's mom wants him to read at least 5 new books over the summer. He went to the book fair and bought the top 5 sellers. How many pages will he read this summer?

2. Meghan is learning how to cook. She went to the book fair to find a cookbook. If there is 1 recipe per page, what is the average cost per recipe for the book she bought?

3. Richard loves to read fiction and realistic fiction books. If he buys all of the fiction and realistic fiction books on the top sellers list, how much will he spend?

4. Pam got $30.00 for her birthday. She wants to spend it at the book fair. What is the maximum number of books she can buy within her budget?

5. Rodney is a big fan of Johnny Sailor. He wants to purchase as many copies of his book as possible to have autographed. How many copies can he buy with $27.00?
   a. 9   c. 11
   b. 10   d. 12

6. How many books on the list are in the range of 50–100 pages?

7. Luis loves to read. He vows to read all 15 books on the top sellers list. He decides to read them in order from longest to shortest. Which book will he read in the middle?

8. Mrs. Morris has many class pets. Her students want to buy her all of the books about animals on the top 15 list. How much money will they need?

9. Mrs. Hill is purchasing books for the school library. About how much would it cost to buy all of the fiction, nonfiction, and realistic fiction books?
   a. $57.00   c. $68.00
   b. $63.00   d. $72.00

10. Principal Bland wants to buy each teacher a copy of *Best Games to Play Inside* because the playground is under construction. There are 25 teachers in the school, but 6 of them already have copies of the book. How much money will he spend?

11. Mrs. Anderson knows that fiction books are popular with her students. However, they do not like realistic fiction. She wants to buy books from the list. What percentage of the top 15 sellers are fiction?
    a. 5%   c. 15%
    b. 10%   d. 20%

Name _____

Buy the Book

Use the top 15 sellers list to answer the questions.

1. Ronetta earns $5.15 an hour working at the book fair. She wants to purchase *Taking Pictures of Your Pets, One Mountain at a Time*, and *There's Something Fuzzy Under My Bed*. How many full hours will she need to work to make her purchase?

2. When the book fair committee is choosing books to sell at the book fair, they want to be sure to have both long and short books. They want the average number of pages to be 85-90 pages. What is the average page count for the top 15 sellers? (Round to the nearest 10th.)

3. The book fair committee wants the average book price to be no greater than $7.00. Did the books on the top 15 sellers list make this goal?

4. When choosing books for the book fair, the committee uses data from the top 15 sellers to choose books for the next year. What is the mode for this year's page count?

5. Mr. Fisher wants to buy one of each of the top 10 sellers for his reading center. He has $80.00 left in his budget. How much over or under his budget will he be after purchasing the 10 books?

6. Miss Carras took 15 students to the local historical museum. Each student read *Roger Goes on a Field Trip* before the trip. Altogether, how many pages did the 15 students read before the trip?
   a. 15   c. 750
   b. 50   d. 1,575

7. Mrs. Maready levels all of her classroom books according to page count. If the range for her lowest group is 25-50 pages, how many books on the top 15 sellers list can her lowest group read?

8. Mrs. Walkush is making a pie chart about the genres of the 6 best-selling books. Help her with her presentation by drawing a pie chart that shows the top 6 sellers grouped by genre. Label each section with a fraction.

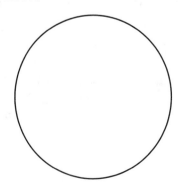

Buy the Book

The Picture:

The picture is a list of the top 15 sellers at a book fair. The list includes titles, genres, number of pages, and prices for the books.

Teacher Notes:

Many story problems require more than one operation to be used when solving the problem. Explain that reading the entire problem before starting calculations is key to solving a multi-step problem. Teach students the following steps to solve a multi-step problem:

1. Identify needed information to solve a problem by looking for key words that determine the necessary operation.
2. Write a number sentence.
3. Discard any extraneous information from the problem.
4. Determine what operation must be completed first, then solve that operation.
5. Solve the second step by using an additional number sentence with the correct operation.
6. Determine the reasonableness of solutions.

Students can remember the definition of each of these terms by using word play.

- The word *mode* sounds like the word *most*. The *mode* is the number that appears most often in a list.
- The *median* is the middle number in a list of numbers that has been put in order. A grass or concrete median divides a road. Tell students to remember the sentence, "*In order* to cross the road, stop *halfway* on the *median*."
- To remember that *mean* is the same as *average*, tell students to remember the sentence, "The *average* bully is *mean*."

Extension Activities:

1. Have a book exchange in your classroom. Students can bring books from home that they have already read and exchange them for books their classmates have read. Have students paper clip an index card inside each book and label it with the book title and owner. Then, when students exchange books, have them sign and date the cards. Collect the cards to track which students have the books now.
2. If you have a book sale at your school, have students keep track of the titles and prices of the books they buy. As a class, figure out top sellers for your class.
3. Using the prices from the previous activity, have students figure out percentages of money spent at the book fair based on certain factors, such as genre, page count, etc. Explain that schools receive a percentage of the money when a book fair comes to a school.
4. Have students collect old books from family and friends to sell at a used book sale. Use the proceeds to buy new books for the classroom library at an upcoming book sale.

CD-104025 • Real-World Math

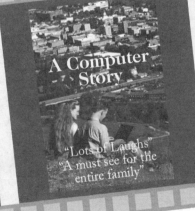

Movies by Mail

Use the mail-order movie advertisement to answer the questions.

1. Larry is a member of the More Movies Club. He is buying *Pirates of the Lost Islands* this month. Including shipping, what is his total?

2. Keisha just decided to join the More Movies Club. For her first purchase, she is buying *Techno Wizard, Road Rash,* and *A Holiday Story.* How much will her first bill be when she joins?

3. Jon is not in the movie club. He orders *Road Rash* and *The Seaside Six.* Claire is in the club. She is ordering the same 2 movies. What will each of them pay? Is it a better deal for Jon to join the club?

4. In a typical month, the More Movies Club gets 50 new members. How much does Mail Order Movies collect in membership fees?
   a. $50.00   c. $150.00
   b. $50.50   d. $500.00

5. Amber is a member of the movie club. She is ordering *Pirates of the Lost Islands, Road Rash,* and *The Seaside Six.* Michael is joining the club this month. He is ordering the same 3 movies. How much will Amber pay? How much will Michael pay? Who is getting a better deal?

6. Kelly is a member of the More Movies Club. She orders 3 copies of *Techno Wizard* to give as gifts. Eric is not in the club and wants to order 4 copies of *A Computer Story* for his friends. Who pays more and what is the difference in their totals?

7. Lamont wants to order *The Seaside Six, A Computer Story,* and *Pirates of the Lost Islands.* He is not a club member but is considering joining. If he joins this month, what will he pay? If he doesn't join, what will he pay? Should Lamont join the movie club?

8. Sara has $20.00 to spend. She is not a club member. How many different movies can she buy?

9. Bart bought 2 movies for a total of $21.90 including shipping. He is not a club member. Which movie combinations could he have bought?

10. Kia joined the More Movies Club. Her first month, she bought *The Seaside Six, Techno Wizard,* and *Pirates of the Lost Islands.* Her second month, she bought *Road Rash, A Computer Story,* and *A Holiday Story.* How much did she pay for both months?

Movies by Mail

Use the mail-order movie advertisement to answer the questions.

1. Jenny is not a club member. She receives $4.00 for allowance each week. How many weeks will she need to save her money if she wants to buy *The Seaside Six*?

2. Frank is a club member. Last month, he bought *Techno Wizard, Road Rash,* and *A Holiday Story.* How much was his bill?

3. Mail-Order Movies wants to know which movies are making the largest profit among non-club members. In 1 month, it sold 25 copies of *The Seaside Six* and 75 copies of *A Computer Story.* Which movie brought in more money?

4. *Road Rash* is this month's best-selling movie among non-club members. It has sold 300 copies so far. The second best-seller among non-club members is *Techno Wizard.* It has sold 250 copies. Which movie has brought in more money and by how much?

5. Mail-Order Movies makes a 60% profit for every movie it sells. If someone buys 2 copies of *Pirates of the Lost Islands* at full price, about how much is the company's profit?
   a. $6.00   c. $18.00
   b. $12.00   d. $19.90

6. If Mail-Order Movies makes 60% profit for every movie sold at full price, would it make a greater profit selling 10 copies of *Techno Wizard* or 19 copies of *A Holiday Story*?

7. Mail-Order Movies likes to keep a variety of prices on its movie list. To do this, it tries to keep the average movie price between $8.00 and $10.00. Did the company accomplish its goal with the movies on this month's flyer? What is the average cost of all movies rounded to the nearest cent?

8. What is a better deal for a non-club member: buying *A Holiday Story* and *Techno Wizard* or buying *Pirates of the Lost Islands* and *A Computer Story*?

9. Laura is a huge fan of Paul Slater and Julia Robertson. If she has been a club member for 6 months, what will she pay to buy their new movies?

10. Adam is a new club member. He decides to buy the 3 most expensive movies. Rachel is not a club member, and she is buying the 3 least expensive movies. Who is spending more money?

Movies by Mail

The Picture:

The picture is an advertisement for mail-order movies. There are six movies on the page that are available for different prices. They have item numbers and short blurbs to describe them. Members are eligible for special rates by joining the movie club for a one-time $10.00 fee. The first month a person joins, she is able to buy three movies for 99¢. After the first month, members must purchase at least one movie per month, but at a price of only $7.95. The discount applies to the highest priced movie. There is a $1.00 shipping and processing fee for each movie purchased.

Teacher Notes:

Most problems on the page are multi-step problems in which all information in the problems is necessary to find the answers. Model decoding a problem with students. For example, explain that it is important to know whether a person is a member because it affects the prices the person will pay. Students should include the membership fee for new members only. The shipping and processing fee is to be added to each movie, whether the person is a member or not. For example, if a new member gets the 3 movies for a total of 99¢, they are still charged an additional $1.00 per movie for shipping and processing. Additionally, they are charged the one-time $10.00 membership fee. Therefore, a new member will pay a minimum of $13.99 for the first three movies she receives. Remind students that existing members get any one movie for $7.95, therefore, if they choose two movies with a list price of $12.95 and $6.95, they will only pay $7.95 for the movie with the $12.95 list price.

Discuss with students the financial advantages and disadvantages of ordering from a movie, book, or CD club. While the initial savings seem to be a great deal, many people are required to buy merchandise they may not necessarily want. The wording in the advertisement may be written to make the consumer think he is getting a better deal than what is actually being offered. For example, the consumer is required to purchase at least one movie per month, yet he may not want any of a particular month's offerings. He is still required to purchase a movie that month, therefore he is paying for unwanted goods. This is how mail-order companies are assured to make money each month.

Extension Activities:

1. Make a mail-order catalog math center. Bring in a variety of mail-order catalogs, such as clothing or electronics catalogs. Laminate the order forms and provide write-on/wipe-away markers. Post questions for students to answer by filling out the catalog order forms. When their answers have been checked, students may erase what they have written on the order forms.
2. Have students bring in advertisements from newspapers and magazines that have book and movie clubs to join. Have students figure the cost of the membership fees and required purchases for each club. Have them present their findings.
3. Bring in advertisements or pamphlets from national movie rental companies. Have the class use a Venn diagram to compare unlimited movie rentals in stores to rent-by-mail movie programs. Using student surveys, have students find the best plans for different consumer needs.

City of **Zornville**
Places of interest around town

Mall

School

2 miles

3 miles

Ballpark

8 miles

5 miles

7 miles

10 miles

8 miles

Downtown

5 miles

Museum

7 miles

Library

4 miles

Zoo

6 miles

6 miles

N
W E
S

* Map not to scale

Taxi Fare

Initial Charge	$2.00
Per 1/3 Mile	30¢
Per Minute Stopped or Slow Traffic	10¢
Night Surcharge	50¢

© Carson-Dellosa • CD-104025

Hailing a Taxi

Use the taxi fare rates and map to answer the questions.

1. Mary went from the zoo to the mall through downtown. There was no traffic. How much was her taxi fare?

2. Jamal went from the museum to downtown. He sat in stopped traffic for 10 minutes. What did he pay?

3. Zelda went from the zoo to the ballpark. She asked the driver to go by the museum. How much did she have to pay the driver if she added a $1.00 tip?

4. Gina works at the mall. After the mall closed at 10:00 P.M., she took a taxi to her apartment next to the library. What was her taxi fare?

5. Tevin works downtown. He takes a taxi to pick up his children, then take them to the ballpark. There is no traffic, but the taxi had to wait for 5 minutes in the school pick-up line. What is the total fare on the meter?

6. Noel is at the library. He needs to go to the mall. There is an accident on the route to the mall. If the taxi's radio says that there will be a 20-minute delay, will it be less expensive to wait on the direct route or to pass through downtown?

7. Last week, Don's taxi picked up a total of 12 people. Altogether, he drove 60 miles and spent 15 minutes in traffic. About how much did Don earn for all of the fares?

8. Elizabeth has to stay late at the library to research a report. She is supposed to meet her friends at the ballpark at 10:00 P.M. The roads downtown are closed for construction. With no traffic, which route is cheaper?
   a. library-zoo-museum-ballpark
   b. library-mall-school-ballpark

9. Every Tuesday night, Sheila drives Mrs. Liberman round trip from her home next to the museum to the mall. In a month with 4 Tuesdays, how much does Mrs. Liberman pay for her trip through downtown?

10. Three friends are meeting at the zoo this morning. Hannah takes a taxi from the library, Zoe takes a taxi from the museum, and Carla passes through downtown from the ballpark. Carla sits in stopped traffic for 6 minutes. What is each girl's fare?

Hailing a Taxi

Use the taxi fare rates and map to answer the questions.

1. Jenika is visiting the city. She has never been to Zornville before, so she decides to take a sightseeing tour around the perimeter of the city. How far did Jenika travel?

2. If Jenika only encountered traffic for 7 minutes of her ride, how much was the taxi fare for her tour?

3. Ebony calls the taxi company to find out the shortest route from the mall to the library with a short stop at the school. How many miles is the shortest route?

4. On the first Monday of the month, the taxi company has a 5% discount on night travel, excluding the initial $2.00 charge. With the discount, how much would it cost for a trip from the zoo to the ballpark via downtown?

5. On the same Monday night, Marshall travels from the ballpark to the mall. With no traffic, what is the least amount he could pay?

6. DeWayne went from the museum to the library with no traffic. Sasha went from the museum to the library with 5 minutes of traffic. How much more did Sasha pay than DeWayne?

7. A taxi driver wants to make the most money possible for the taxi company. What is the most expensive route from the zoo to the ballpark without going through downtown?

8. If the taxi driver takes the most direct route instead of the longest route from the zoo to the ballpark, how much money would his passengers save?
   a. $8.10   c. $18.90
   b. $10.80   d. $19.80

9. Shawn calls a taxi to pick him up at the museum. The driver calls Shawn's cell phone when he arrives, then starts the meter. If Shawn does not come out for 20 minutes, then rides to the library, how much of his fare charge was the waiting fee?
   a. $1.00   c. $1.75
   b. $1.50   d. $2.00

10. Kaleb goes to his after-school job at the zoo. He usually takes the bus for $1.50, but he missed the bus. He takes a taxi so that he won't be late. He avoids downtown to save time. How much more did he have to pay for missing the bus?
    a. $14.90   c. $16.40
    b. $16.00   d. $18.00

Hailing a Taxi

The Picture:
The picture is a taxi that displays its rates for fares. There is a map that has various points of interest in the town and the mileage between the points.

Teacher Notes:
Remind students that there is a $2.00 initial fee just for getting into the taxi. Every time a question asks what the fare is, students should make sure they add this initial fee to the total.

If students do not live in a large city, the idea of taking a taxi for transportation may be foreign to them. Discuss different kinds of transportation in rural and urban areas. For example, in New York City it is very expensive to have a car (parking is at a premium), so most people take taxis, buses, or the subway. It is easy to locate a taxi in the city, and the taxi takes the person exactly to the destination.

Using the rate sign on the taxi and the information below, teach students to calculate fares by determining the price per mile.
1. There are $^3/_3$ in every mile, so multiply 30¢ by three. (3 x $0.30 = $0.90)
2. Multiply $0.90 by each mile traveled.
3. Add the $2.00 initial cost.
   - Add 10¢ for every minute the taxi was stopped or in slow traffic
   - Add the night surcharge if necessary.

Extension Activities:
1. Have students make up their own problems using the taxi rate sign. Have students trade problems or post the problems on a bulletin board for students to solve when they are finished with their math class work.
2. Have students calculate what their fares would be if they had to take taxis to school each day.
3. Have students calculate the tip for each problem on the worksheets. Remind students that 15% is the customary tip amount.
4. Have students research different forms of public transportation in your area.

Sale on Saturday

Use the sale advertisement to answer the questions.

1. Ginger needs athletic tees for gym class. How much money can she save if she buys 6 athletic tees?

2. Mrs. Tate wants to save additional money during the sale. What percent will she save if she opens a Schoolman's credit card account?

3. Mona bought a leather jacket and opened a credit card account. How much did she pay for her new leather jacket?
   a. $49.99   c. $44.99
   b. $81.00   d. $130.50

4. Mr. Averitt wanted to get gifts for his 4 sons. He may buy 1 gift for them to share if it saves him money. Which is more expensive, 1 train set or 4 scooters?

5. Bonnie's mom bought her a new coat for her vacation to Alaska. What fraction of the regular price did she pay by going to the sale?
   a. $\frac{1}{2}$ c. $\frac{1}{3}$
   b. $\frac{1}{6}$ d. $\frac{2}{3}$

6. Jared has $100.00. Can he afford a bike and a CD player from Schoolman's?

7. Sarah and her friends decided to buy matching backpacks. She is going to Schoolman's to buy them. If she bought 3 backpacks, the total she paid would be between which price range?

8. Lola has $40.00 to buy all of her back-to-school clothes. What is the largest number of skirts and tops she could buy?

9. Mrs. Harris bought the scooter that was originally the most expensive in the store. What percentage did she end up saving by waiting until Saturday to buy the scooter? (Round to the nearest whole number.)

10. What is the greater percent of savings: a leather jacket that was originally $145.00 or a tee that was originally $34.00?

11. Guillermo needed a helmet to go with his new bicycle. If he bought the least expensive helmet and a bike, how much was his purchase?

12. Roberto got to the sale 25 minutes after it started. How long will he be able to shop during the sale hours?

Name _____

Sale on Saturday

Use the sale advertisement to answer the questions.

1. If a Super Pretendo video game was originally $30.00, how much is it at the Schoolman's Saturday Sale?

2. On Saturday, the Zapitron game was on sale for 50% off. If the original price was $24.00, how much are 3 Zapitrons on Saturday?

3. Mrs. Acree loves a bargain, but she does not like credit cards. What is the greatest percentage of savings she could receive on a leather jacket during the sale? (Round to the nearest tenth.)

4. Fred's father is a train engineer. He bought his son a new train set. What percentage did he save at the sale?
   a. 33%   c. 54%
   b. 35%   d. 70%

5. If Casey's mom bought him the most expensive bike helmet, what was the original price?

6. Marcella bought 2 athletic tees and a TV on sale. How much money did she save?
   a. $173.03   c. $144.97
   b. $318.00   d. $182.00

7. All scooters are $29.99. If Abby buys 2 scooters, what is the greatest amount she could save from the original price?

8. Tammy wanted to buy a variety of skirts and tops for her first week of school. What is the range of the prices for girls tops and skirts?

9. Joaquin looked at TVs on Thursday night. He bought 2 TVs at the Schoolman's Saturday Sale. How much did he save by waiting until Saturday to make his purchase?

10. On Saturday, bike helmets are an extra 50% off. If total savings are 60%, what was the original sale percentage?

11. It is a 30-minute drive to get to Schoolman's. Rachel wants to be there 10 minutes before the sale starts. What time should she leave her house?

12. After the sale on Saturday ended, the price of the 13" TVs went up 20% from the sale price. What is the new price of a 13" TV?

Sale on Saturday

The Picture:

The picture is a sale advertisement. At the bottom of the advertisement, there is an offer to apply for a store credit card to receive an additional 10% off of a purchase.

Teacher Notes:

Explain to students that discounts allow people to save money. To see how much money can be saved, have students figure out the full price of an item, then have them subtract the amount of the discounted price.

When working with money amounts, remind students to line up decimal points before adding, subtracting, or multiplying.

Explain how to convert decimals to fractions and percents:

- Fraction to a decimal: Divide the numerator by the denominator.
- Decimal to a fraction: Remove the decimal point and write the number as the numerator. The denominator should be a multiple of 10, depending on the place the last digit of the decimal occupies. For example, if the decimal is 0.235, then the denominator is 1,000 because the last digit of the decimal occupies the thousandths place. The fraction can then be reduced to lowest terms.
- Fraction to a percent: Divide the numerator by the denominator, then move the decimal point two places to the right.
- Decimal to a percent: Move the decimal two places to the right.

Extension Activities:

1. Bring in items and attach price tags to them. Place them in a center. Each week, display a different discount percentage. Have students keep track of the prices they would pay for the items each week. Then, have each student choose one item and make a line graph of the fluctuation in price over a one month period.
2. Collect store circulars from a Sunday newspaper. Have students compare prices of the same items in different stores. For example, most grocery stores or drugstores have sales on soda, candy, and shampoo. Have students choose items common to the circulars provided and determine which store has the best price overall or if it is more economical to purchase the items separately from a variety of stores.
3. Write on the board a certain amount of money to spend, such as $100.00. Post a local sales circular for students to use. Have them list what they would buy and how much it would cost on sale. Have partners check each other's work.
4. Ask parents or guardians to donate items for students to sell at school. Let students price the items and then post discounts. Allow students to work with partners to calculate merchandise totals and correct change for customers.

Garden A

Garden B

Garden C

Garden D

fountain

1 ft. = 0.3 m

■ = planted area

0' 5' 10' 15' 20' 25' 30'

0' 5' 10' 15' 20'

Gorgeous Garden

Use the garden blueprint to answer the questions.

1. Mr. Kennedy wanted to make each of the 4 gardens equal. What is the area of each garden?

2. Mr. Kennedy measured each of the gardens correctly. What is the total garden area not including the pathways and fountain?

3. The paths must be at least 3 feet 3 inches wide for wheelchair access. How must the current paths be adjusted to allow a wheelchair to be able to maneuver on the paths?

4. The fountain in the center of the garden must be measured before it is placed. What is the area of land where the fountain will be placed?

5. The volunteers are roping off the area of the entire garden. What is the area of the entire blueprint?

6. How many meters of rope did the volunteers use to rope off the outside perimeter of the entire garden?

7. Mr. Kennedy is buying the plants for garden B first. What is the area allotted for plants in garden B?

8. When planning his gardens, Mr. Kennedy wanted to make 2 gardens congruent. Which garden is congruent to garden A?
   a. none
   b. garden B
   c. garden C
   d. garden D

9. Mr. Kennedy was talking to the man who is delivering mulch for the gardens. He needed to know how much mulch he needed to put around the plants. What percentage of garden A is plants? (Round to the nearest 10th.)

10. What percentage of garden B is plants? (Round to the nearest 10th.)

11. When buying concrete for the gardens' paths, Mr. Kennedy needed to buy 1 bag of concrete for every 10 square feet of path. What is the square footage of the path area?

12. Mr. Kennedy is on his way to the home improvement store to buy the concrete. How many bags of concrete will he need to buy?

Name _____

Gorgeous Garden

Use the garden blueprint to answer the questions.

1. The fountain will be the focal point of the garden. What percent of the entire garden is the fountain? (Round to the nearest tenth.)

2. The paths should not take up as much area as the garden. What fraction of the entire garden is paths?

3. What fraction of the entire garden is garden C and garden D?

4. Mr. Hatfield wants to know if he needs more concrete for the paths or more plants. Which takes up more area, the paths or the plants in gardens A and B?

5. Tabitha guessed that there are more plants in gardens B and C. Alan guessed that there are more plants in gardens B and D. Who guessed correctly?

6. If 33% of the area planted in garden A is roses, how many square feet in garden A are roses? (Round to the nearest whole number.)
   a. 17.0   c. 17.16
   b. 17.1   d. 18.0

7. If $\frac{3}{4}$ of the plants in garden D are daisies, how many square feet contain daisies?

8. Mr. Hatfield is planting 8 kinds of flowers in the 4 gardens, and he wants to use an equal number of square feet for each flower. How many square feet will each type of flower occupy? List a fraction and a decimal for your answer.

9. If 1 square foot equals 0.3 square meter, how many square meters is the entire area of garden A?

10. How many total square meters are covered with plants?

11. The gardener wants to put a border of bricks along the outside edge of the entire garden, omitting the pathway entrances. If one brick is 8 inches long, how many bricks will she need?

12. Mr. Hatfield is considering placing a pattern of bricks in the concrete path. The standard dimensions of one brick is $3\frac{1}{2}$" x $2\frac{1}{4}$" x 8". What is the volume of the brick in cubic inches?

Gorgeous Garden

The Picture:

The picture is a blueprint for a garden. There is a fountain in the center and four intersecting paths that meet at the fountain. Each shaded square represents one square foot of planted area. Light areas are dirt or mulch areas. There are four gardens that are labeled A–D. Gardens A and D are congruent, and gardens B and C are congruent. There is a number grid on the x- and y-axis to make counting easier.

Teacher Notes:

Teach students to find the area of a garden, planted area, or path by counting the number of squares it contains. Explain that two triangles equal one square unit. When trying to find an area within another area, have students find the area of the entire garden, then subtract the area of a given planted area. The difference is the remaining area of the garden.

Explain to students that *congruent* means the same size and same shape.

Extension Activities:

1. Have students use a garden catalog to price how much it would cost to purchase bricks, plants, and a fountain for the blueprint.
2. Have students use graph paper to design a garden for school. If possible, plan for the garden to contain a path or bench.
3. Give each student a piece of graph paper. Write various perimeters for a garden on the board. Include perimeters for a path and planting areas. Have students use the graph paper to create all possible garden areas with the given perimeters.
4. Create a 15 x 15 unit garden. When it is complete, copy it on a transparency. Then, give students graph paper and a list of directions to recreate the same garden using vocabulary that describes location, area, perimeter, and congruency. Show students the transparency and have them use it to check their work.
5. Invite a professional landscaper to talk to students. Have her talk about the planning and purchasing procedures for home and business landscaping. Ask the speaker to bring in different blueprints and layouts, an itemized price list of plants she typically uses, and pictures of completed gardens for students to see.
6. Use the information from Caring for Roses (page 13) to plant and grow roses in a garden at school.
7. Encourage students to adopt a community garden in the school's neighborhood. Students can help create a neighborhood garden if there is not already one in existence. Make sure students' plans for the neighborhood garden accommodate people with special needs.

House for Sale by Owner

1059 Hawthorne Road
Phone: 555-5309

Age	built 1928
Levels	2
Area in Square Feet	1,450
Area in Square Meters	134.71
List Price	$159,500
Bedrooms	3
Baths	2 full
Sewer	city/public
Water	city/public
Basement	yes/unfinished-dirt
Lot Size	50' x 254' x 50' x 254'
Lot Size	15.24 m x 77.42 m x 15.24 m x 77.42 m
Flooring	tile, wood, carpet
Parking	shared driveway/3-car lot
Misc.	porch, fenced lot, landscaping

Type	single-family home
Subdivision	Lyman Estates
Style	bungalow
Exterior	brick
Acreage	0.29 acres
Cooling	central
Heat	furnace
Fuel	natural gas
Fireplace	1
Garage	2-car, attached

Room Information

Room:	Level:	Dimensions:	
Living Room	main	17' x 20'	(5.18 m x 6.10 m)
Dining Room	main	12' x 14'	(3.66 m x 4.27 m)
Kitchen	main	10' x 17'	(3.05 m x 5.18 m)
Office	main	13' x 12'	(3.96 m x 3.66 m)
Master Bedroom	upper	15' x 13'	(4.57 m x 3.96 m)
Second Bedroom	main	12' x 12'	(3.66 m x 3.66 m)
Third Bedroom	main	12' x 11'	(3.66 m x 3.35 m)

For Sale by Owner

Use the house flyer to answer the questions.

List rooms' areas in square feet. List them from largest to smallest.

1. _____

2. _____

3. _____

4. _____

5. _____

6. _____

7. _____

8. Scott is looking for a house with a lot that is at least 1,200 square meters. What is the area of the lot in square meters? (Round your answer to the nearest hundredth.)

9. The current owners have lived in the house since it was 14 years old. If it is 2006, how long have they lived in the house?

10. If bathrooms, hallways, closets, storage area, and side porch are figured in the overall area, how much space do they occupy in square feet? In square meters?

11. Mr. Brykczynski knows that the lot is .29 acres but he wants to know what that equals in square feet. How large an area is the lot in square feet?

12. Mrs. Barlow does not want a large lawn to mow. If the realtor assures her that only 15% of the lot is lawn, how many square feet are there to mow?

13. Patty wants a brick home because she thinks it is easier to care for than a home that has an aluminum siding exterior. A brick home in Lyman Estates costs $10.00 more per square foot than a home with an aluminum siding exterior. How much more is the home on the flyer than an aluminum siding home with the same square footage?

14. Kendall wants a larger bedroom than her brother. If her parents get the master bedroom, what is the area of the room Kendall wants?

For Sale by Owner

Use the house flyer to answer the questions.

1. Is the area of the three bedrooms smaller or larger than the combined area of the office, dining room, and living room?

2. What fraction of the lot is occupied by the house?

3. What percentage of the lot is occupied by the house? Round to the nearest 10th of a percent.

4. The homes in Lyman Estates are usually priced at $100 per square foot. How much more or less is the Hawthorne house priced per square foot?

5. If the current selling rate in Lyman Estates is $95.00 per square foot, what would be a reasonable offer for the house?

6. It is 2006. If the owners have replaced the roof every 10 years since the house was built, how many roofs has it had?

7. When will the new owners need to replace the roof if the current roof has a 20-year guarantee?

8. The house is for sale by owner. Real estate agents usually make 3% commission for selling a house. If the sellers decide to use an agent and the house sells for the asking price, how much money will they need to pay the agent?

9. The Millers want to buy the house on Hawthorne. They applied for a 20-year loan. The bank charges 5.5% interest in addition to the asking price. How much will the Millers pay for the house?

10. The side porch that is 6' x 8' is not included in the square footage of the house. If the porch were included in the area of the house, what would be the new total square footage of the house?

11. Mark wants to put a king-size bed in the master bedroom. If the bed is 76" x 80", how much area is left in the bedroom? (Round your answer to the nearest hundredth)

12. It costs $1.75 per square foot for new carpet for the living room. How much will the new carpet cost altogether?

For Sale by Owner

The Picture:

The picture is a flyer about a house that is for sale by the owner. It includes information for prospective buyers, such as the price, number of bedrooms and bathrooms, and room size.

Teacher Notes:

To find the area of a room from the given dimensions, have students multiply the room's length by its width. To find the area of the lot, tell students to multiply the length of the lot by the width.

To find the perimeter, have students add the two given dimensions, then multiply the sum by two.

Have students divide the price of the home by the amount of square feet/meters to find the price per square foot/meter.

Tell students that the sum of the given room dimensions is 1,305 ft.^{2} (121.23 m^2). The remaining area of the house is bathrooms, closets, hallways, and storage. The total area listed on the flyer does not include the attached garage.

To determine the amount of interest, have students multiply the interest percentage by the price of the home. Then, have them add the interest to the price of the home.

Extension Activities:

1. Have students bring in flyers from their neighborhoods' real estate books or from real estate Web sites. Have them find the area of each room.
2. Using the flyers from the previous activity, have students figure out what the mortgage payments would be for houses in different price ranges. Have students estimate how much income a person must earn to buy a certain house. (Explain that most banks recommend that a person's monthly salary is three times one month's mortgage payment.) Have students research different interest rates on loans for a 10-, 15-, 20-, or 30-year mortgage to determine how much money can be saved by the home buyer.
3. Assign each student to measure a piece of furniture from his home. Have him bring in the measurements to use for a class project. Record the measurements of one of each type of furniture on the board. Have each student choose one room from the flyer and use graph paper to place "furniture" in the room. Let students determine how many different arrangements can be made in the amount of space given.
4. Request information from various utility companies to find the most cost-efficient way to heat, cool, and supply power to a home. For example, are there advantages to gas, electric, or oil heat sources?
5. Challenge students to determine the monthly mortgage payment. The monthly payment is determined by the total price divided by the number of months it will take to pay for the home. For example, a home that costs $100,000 with 5.5% interest equals $105,500. For a 20-year mortgage (240 months), the monthly house payment would be approximately $439.58.

Answer Key

Right Up Your Alley
Page 6
1. 4
2. Sandra and Roger
3. frame 7; 8 points
4. frame 9; 87 points
5. 117.6
6. 112
7. 27; Fiona and Sandra
8. c.
9. a.
10. 44 points
11. 2 pins
12. 129

Page 7
1. a.
2. c.
3. $10.50
4. $52.50
5. $60.00
6. $102.50
7. $12.50
8. $2.50
9. $110.00
10. Roger
11. $10.00

When Is My Flight?
Page 10
1. 30 minutes
2. 3:30 P.M.
3. 1 hour 25 minutes
4. a.
5. 6:55 P.M.
6. 5:05 P.M.
7. b.
8. 35%
9. c.
10. 1 hour 52 minutes
11. 3 hours 13 minutes

Page 11
1. 200 gates
2. $\frac{1}{5}$
3. 3:35 P.M.
4. flight 41 to Orlando
5. 6:52 P.M.
6. 5:25 P.M.
7. 37 passengers
8. 10% higher
9. 1200 passengers
10. c.

Caring for Roses
Page 14
1. no
2. b.
3. 2 20"-wide holes;
   3 16"-wide holes
4. 130 gallons
5. d.
6. 40 gallons
7. $5\frac{2}{3}$ cups triple super
   phosphate and dolomite;
   34 cups alfalfa pellets
8. c.
9. 30 gallons
10. 3 months

Page 15
1. 15.24 cm
2. 1.9 liters
3. d.
4. 3
5. d.
6. 8 cups
7. 4-6 times
8. 1:1
9. b.
10. 16 inches

Foreign Exchange
Page 18
1. 50.60 reals
2. Iraq; C$12.40
3. $2.00
4. no
5. Franz
6. 65 euros
7. more
8. $10.00
9. no
10. $2.83
11. d.
12. 118.77 baht per hour

Page 19
1. b.
2. gain
3. greater
4. 70.16 pounds
5. NZ$323.26
6. c.
7. yen (Japan) and shilling
   (Kenya)
8. 559.48 rubles
9. Australian dollar
10. Argentina

Batter Up!
Page 22
1. 0.333
2. 0.500
3. 0.370
4. 0.270
5. 0.291
6. 0.250
7. 0.340
8. 0.423
9. 0.436
10. d.

Answer Key

Page 22 (cont.)
11. 110
12. 78
13. Pete
14. 0.357

Page 23
1. Tammy
2. Steve
3. Debbie
4. Carrie
5. 36
6. 84
7. girls
8. Pattie
9. b.
10. 60
11. b.
12. Debbie, David, and Frannie

Let's Do Lunch
Page 26
1. $25.98
2. 10
3. 2
4. $\frac{4}{11}$
5. 9
6. 75%
7. $12.00
8. 2 hamburgers, 1 baked potato, and a chicken deluxe
9. d.
10. c.
11. $\frac{1}{2}$

Page 27
1. a.
2. $13.30
3. $6.10
4. 12
5. d.
6. 2 ounces
7. $2.74
8. c.
9. soup, spaghetti, ice cream ($12.00)
10. 7
11. Answers will vary.

Phone Home
Page 30
1. 6
2. Friendly Wireless
3. 22 minutes
4. c.
5. $240.00
6. 7
7. Susan
8. Joan and Susan
9. d.
10. $6.00
11. $6.00

Page 31
1. 25¢
2. $270.00
3. $11.13
4. $5.67 more
5. 38¢; 25¢; 48¢
6. $66\frac{2}{3}$ minutes
7. 20 minutes
8. $69.60
9. $120.00
10. a.
11. 48¢

Fragrant Fund-Raiser
Page 34
1. d.
2. 20 crocus bulbs
3. no
4. a.
5. 4 dahlia plants
6. 7
7. 4 alliums, 2 crocuses, 1 tulip
8. $32.39
9. yes
10. c.
11. $7.99; $14.99; $18.32
12. $131.93

Page 35
1. $\frac{7}{9}$
2. alliums
3. $13.20
4. 125 bulbs
5. d.
6. $76.00
7. 56%
8. $8.31
9. c.
10. 25 hyacinths and 10 alliums

Buy the Book
Page 38
1. 348
2. 10¢
3. $25.95
4. 5
5. a.
6. 9
7. *Hamsters in Outer Space*

CD-104025 • Real-World Math

Answer Key

Page 38 (cont.)
8. $23.85
9. b.
10. $227.05
11. d.

Page 39
1. 5
2. 85.5
3. no
4. 50
5. $3.40 under
6. c.
7. 5
8.

Movies by Mail
Page 42
1. $8.95
2. $13.99
3. Jon: $23.90;
   Claire: $18.90; yes
4. d.
5. Amber: $29.85;
   Michael:$13.99; Michael
6. Kelly; $1.05
7. $13.99; $32.85; yes
8. 2
9. *Road Rash* and *Techno
   Wizard* or *The Seaside
   Six* and *A Computer
   Story*
10. $37.84

Page 43
1. 4
2. $25.85
3. *A Computer Story*
4. *Techno Wizard* by
   $52.50
5. b.
6. *A Holiday Story*
7. yes; $9.28
8. neither-same deal
9. $18.90
10. Rachel

Hailing a Taxi
Page 46
1. $12.80
2. $7.50
3. $14.70
4. $11.50
5. $12.40
6. direct route
7. $79.50
8. b.
9. $113.60
10. Hannah: $7.40; Zoe:
    $7.40; Carla: $10.70

Page 47
1. 34 miles
2. $33.30
3. 14 miles
4. $10.17
5. $6.75
6. 50¢
7. zoo-library-mall-school-
   ballpark
8. b.
9. d.
10. a.

Sale on Saturday
Page 50
1. $144.06
2. 10%
3. c.
4. train set
5. c.
6. yes
7. $29.97-$74.97
8. 5
9. 67%
10. tee at 70.6% savings
11. $60.98
12. 1 hour 35 minutes

Page 51
1. $15.00
2. $36.00
3. 65.5%
4. b.
5. $51.00
6. a.
7. $120.00
8. $7.48-$13.60
9. $250.02
10. 10%
11. 7:20 A.M.
12. $149.99

Gorgeous Garden
Page 54
1. 121.5 ft.^{2}
2. 486 ft.^{2}
3. increase by 1'3"
4. 14 ft.^{2}
5. 600 ft.^{2}
6. 30 meters
7. 44.5 ft.^{2}
8. d.

Answer Key

Page 54 (cont.)
9. 42.8%
10. 36.6%
11. 100 ft.^{2}
12. 10 bags

Page 55
1. 2.3%
2. $\frac{1}{6}$
3. $\frac{81}{200}$
4. paths
5. Alan
6. a.
7. 39 ft.^{2}
8. 24.125 or $24\frac{1}{8}$ ft.^{2}
9. 36.45 m^2
10. 57.9 m^2
11. 138 bricks
12. 63 in.^{3}

For Sale by Owner
Page 58
1. living room: 340 ft.^{2}
2. master bedroom: 195 ft.^{2}
3. kitchen: 170 ft.^{2}
4. dining room: 168 ft.^{2}
5. office: 156 ft.^{2}
6. second bedroom: 144 ft.^{2}
7. third bedroom: 132 ft.^{2}
8. 1,179.88 m^2
9. 64 years
10. 145 ft.^{2}; 13.44 m^2
11. 12,700 ft.^{2}
12. 1,905 ft.^{2}
13. $14,500.00
14. 144 ft.^{2}

Page 59
1. smaller
2. $\frac{29}{254}$
3. 11.4%
4. $10.00 more
5. $137,750.00
6. 8 roofs
7. 2018
8. $4,785.00
9. $168,272.50
10. 1,498 ft.^{2}
11. 152.78 ft.^{2}
12. $595.00